Will I Look Back?

Robert Downie

PublishAmerica
Baltimore

© 2004 by Robert Downie.
All rights reserved. No part of this book may be reproduced, stored in a retrieval system or transmitted in any form or by any means without the prior written permission of the publishers, except by a reviewer who may quote brief passages in a review to be printed in a newspaper, magazine or journal.

First printing

ISBN: 1-4137-4541-5
PUBLISHED BY PUBLISHAMERICA, LLLP
www.publishamerica.com
Baltimore

Printed in the United States of America

I dedicate this book to Cristy, my true love. Thank you for always standing behind my decisions and for giving me the confidence to do anything. I couldn't have done this without you.

I wish to sincerely thank Publish America for having the vision to publish this book. I also want to say a special thank you to my sister, Cathy Downie; I would not be here today if you weren't there during all of those hard times. Thank you very much to my dad and to Nanny. I know that you will always be there for me in good and in bad.

I would also like to thank Skip Marker and Rick Drews for many years of great friendship. Thank you to the entire Zell family for always making me feel like I'm one of your own. Front cover photo taken by Robert Downie.

Will I Look Back

When I am old, will I look back?
Will I see the path? Will I see the track?
The path that I take will determine my life.
Did I have kids? Did I have a wife?

Was my life happy or was my life grim?
Did I just float or did I swim?
Did I take chances and give it my all?
Did I make it happen or did I drop the ball?

Was I myself or did I wear a mask?
These are deep questions that I now ask.
I want to make sure that I get it all right.
If I was a bird, would I be in flight?

Did I run from my problems or did I stand tall?
Did I climb up that hill or did I fall?
I hope that I stay on the right track.
When I am old, will I look back?

Destined To Be

How do I ask her? What should I say?
When do I ask her? When's the right day?
It all must be perfect, it all must be right.
Should it be daytime or should it be night?

I am so nervous she better say yes.
I am a little bit scared I must also confess.
So here goes nothing, if I don't ask, I won't know.
Well ready or not, here I go.

Just close your eyes and listen to me.
Now open them up when my count hits three.
Look at my hands; I'm down on my knees.
I want you for my wife, I'm asking you please.

Please take this ring and stand by my side.
You look so incredible, a beautiful bride.
Not only my bride but my best friend in life;
We were destined to be man and wife.

Inside Beauty

It's the beauty inside that I love to see.
That by far is most important to me.
Just to know that you will always be there,
No one in this world could ever compare.

I close my eyes and I think of your kiss.
Every minute apart it's you that I miss.
You have touched my heart in a special way.
I thank god that I found you every day.

My body quivers when I feel your touch.
You smell so good I love you so much.
You have an angelic smile and such a kind soul.
You are all that I think about, I'm losing control.

The future is there for you and for me.
I see a dog, a house, and a large family.
A couple of kids to pass on our love.
A lifetime of happiness is all I think of.

It's the beauty inside that I love to see.
Nothing more matters to me.
I lit some candles and then I blew.
I made my wish and it came true.

Lost Innocence

September eleventh was the day,
We all were stunned with nothing to say.
Emotions ran wild, all innocence was lost.
Our patriotism ran high but what a great cost.

They had an evil idea to pull America apart.
Instead, we all came together and shared the same heart.
Although none of us will ever be the same.
We all helped each other without even knowing a name.

All of the people that gave up their life;
To help another man, or child, or wife.
It was the worst disaster we have ever seen.
We are all one world so why be so mean.

Now it has been 60 days since the crash.
Nothing is left there but steel and ash.
This is something we will never forget.
But you pulled us together so you will regret.

Our country is powerful and our country is strong.
War is devastating and terrorism is wrong.
I close my eyes and still see the blast.
This is a memory that will forever last.

Working It All Away

We don't ever take the time to enjoy life anymore.
But isn't that the goal that we all strive for?
Most of our adult life we work all away;
Because we can't enjoy life without that pay.

Everything in this world revolves around money.
That is something that I find very funny.
We made up the rules; we made it this way.
Did we know then that we would work everyday?

Can't change it now it will only get worse.
I think that working is really a curse.
Can't spend time with your kids or your wife;
But isn't that the best part of living our life?

We don't take the time to enjoy life anymore.
Life is something that I really adore.
With all of the beautiful things in the world to see;
To spend my life working just isn't for me.

For You, Dad

Every year on this day,
There are too many words for me to say.
How do I thank you for all you have done?
A new hammer or screwdriver or maybe a nail gun.

You're always there to help me with my car.
So in my eyes, you're my biggest star.
So how do I start to pay you back?
Some new craftsman tools all in a stack.

I guess what it is I am trying to say.
Is I need to thank you every day.
Cause if it was not for you, I would not be.
So HAPPY FATHER'S DAY to you from me.

April Fool's

April Fool's is a very strange day;
A day full of tricks and jokes that we play.
One day out of the year that we don't feel so old.
But on this day don't believe what you're told.

If you're not careful, it will happen to you.
And once it does, you'll play it, too.
So how do we know what's real or fake?
Put yourself on guard for your own sake.

So what is the best trick that I have seen?
It was not funny; it was very mean.
Someone called and said that my friend had died.
I took it for real and so I had cried.

How did I know if it was fake or real?
It ended up fake but here's the deal.
Please have fun and go play your tricks;
Mess with people and get your kicks.

But when you go to choose what joke to play.
Please be smart and watch what you say.
This is day that should only be fun.
So watch your back until this day is done.

Meaning of Being Rich

All I want is to be rich,
Rich in mind, rich in spirit.

All I want is to be rich,
Rich in love, not to fear it.

If I had these few things,
Finally then rich I would be.

The One

All I want is to meet my soul mate.
But now I worry that it is too late.
Have I blown that one chance?
To find that one special romance.

Would I know if I have missed,
That special one to hold and kiss?
Is there more than one for us?
Or is it just a feeling of lust?

I hope one day I find that one.
When I do, I will be stunned.
As time goes on, I start to think.
I pray I didn't miss her when I blinked.

Change

I'm not the man I used to be.
I've completely changed this I see.
But have I changed for better or worse?
Am I blessed or am I cursed?

I think that I made a very good change.
Every change is a little strange.
I questioned the cons and I questioned at the pros;
I answered with yes's and I answered with no's.

It wasn't easy but now I'm here.
My future is bright; there's no more fear.
If I could only get that one good break,
The future is there for me to take.

Amazing

It's all I can think about; it's all I can say.
It's the only thing that I wish for every day.
There's nothing else that could make me as happy.
Love is in the air that's why I sound sappy.

You know how it feels when you find that one.
Everyday is brighter and everyday is more fun.
I smile all day long; I smile through the night.
I only saw one thing—it was love at first sight.

From that one day and that very first kiss.
Every minute apart, it's you that I miss.
You have amazing eyes and a beautiful soul.
Just writing this down, I'm losing control.

My heart beats faster when you come near.
With you by my side, there's nothing I fear.
Grab you close and make love all night long.
You and I, baby, were meant to belong.

I can't explain it but I feel like a king.
I love you so much I just want to sing.
Sing out loud so everyone can hear.
You are my sweetie I love you, my dear.

Our Children First

I have something that I must say.
There are many young children in harm's way.
If I could change the world, this is what I would do.
Start by taking care of our country before you.

Stop this crazy war that we're now stuck in.
Put that money towards our own sin.
Take care of our own before we fix yours.
Fix the poverty in our country and open some doors.

Give our own kids the chance they need.
Things can't grow if you don't plant those seeds.
Your country might need help that I understand,
But why help you when we can't meet our own demand.

Get our country straight and lead by example.
Help other countries by showing them a sample.
This is how to do it; we showed you it works.
Now it's time to stand up and do it yourself, you jerks.

I Wonder If

I now see that we won't be.
I wonder if you loved me.
I think of what we could be,
If you would have chosen me.

I now see that we won't be;
Spending our time happily.
Together just you and me,
I just want you to be happy.

Another time another place,
To touch your heart and kiss your face.
I wonder what your thoughts might be.
I wonder if you love me.

Give It a Chance

I see the glare when I look in your eyes;
Brighter than the sun in the sky.
When you smile, my whole body goes numb.
I cannot think straight I feel like I'm dumb.

Just for that chance to kiss your lips.
My whole body shakes, even my hips.
I grab your hand and put it on to my chest.
You can feel my heart race and why I can't rest.

The love is there for you and for me.
Please give it a chance, let's try and let's see.
I really don't think that I am wrong.
I knew it when I first saw you that we belong.

Bring Out a Smile

Sometimes it's hard to bring out a smile.
Since the last one, it's been quite a while.
Selfish is one thing that's easy to be.
Selfish is one thing that can be hard to see.

Depression is something that I have faced.
Depression is something I thought I erased.
But every so often, it tries to come back.
I try so hard to stay on that positive track.

With the day to day grind, life can get hard.
If life was school, I'd have a bad report card.
I try so hard but things just don't work out.
The only relief is to scream and shout.

But then I take a second and I look around.
There are millions worse that I have found.
Millions are worse, so why am I sad?
I guess my life is not all that bad.

Greatness

Every once in a while, I feel a little insane.
Every once in a while, I walk in the rain.
Sometimes I sit and I wonder, "Why me?"
Sometimes I think about who I'd like to be.

What if it was a different life for me?
Would I be the same or who would I be?
What would I change if I could?
And how would I know if I should?

I think I have done all that I can.
I want to be the very best man.
Am I insane because of my thoughts?
I am not perfect; I do have faults.

I'm surrounded by greatness everywhere I look.
But this is the path that I took.
I know someday I will be a star.
I see the future and it's not that far.

I make the choices, and I control my fate.
I can use my brain and not fall for that bait.
I see greatness within my reach.
It's mine for the taking, but it's different for each.

Dream State

When I wake up, I look to see.
If this is real, could it be?
But what if this is a dream,
Endless like a mountain stream?

I pinch myself just to see.
I feel no pain, so dream it must be.
Now I must make my move.
It is my love that I must prove.

Once I do, you will see.
Just how much you mean to me.
Soon you will see that I am not wrong.
I know you feel it because it is strong.

The future is there for you and me.
So take my hand so we can be,
Next to each other all day and all night.
I'm telling you I love you, I'm telling you tonight.

A World Away

I know that all of the pieces fit.
So that is the reason we must commit.
I love you and you love me.
Let's give it a chance, let's try it and see.

I know that we have both been through hard times.
But when I close my eyes, I see all of the signs.
I love being with you; all of our times are great.
So let's take that next step no reason to wait.

I know you might be nervous but so am I.
The saying goes you never know unless you try.
This is more than just passion, this is love.
This is what all great romances are made of.

So let's leave today; let's go right now.
We'll make it some way; we'll make it somehow.
Drop what you're doing and leave it all behind.
A small deserted island is what we will find.

Together in peace just you and me;
Ocean all around us nothing else to see.
Forget about the bills and live off the land.
All day to swim in the water, and play in the sand

Our kids would grow up without all this crime.
Just sitting back, enjoying life with nothing on our mind.
My wife by my side, our kids playing in the sand.
Now you tell me, is this too much to demand?

Call Me

Call me nuts, call me crazy.
Call me boring, call me lazy.
Call me at night, call me in the day.
Call me now, call me right away.

Call me a fish, call me a seal.
Call me whatever it is that you feel.
I don't care about what you say.
I don't like you anyway.

Call me stupid, call me fat.
Call me a dog, call me a cat.
Call me a pig, call me an owl.
Say I smell, call me foul.

If you think it's fun, then call me a name.
Go right ahead and play that game.
If you would open your eyes, you would see.
Sticks and stones might break my bones, but names will never hurt me.

Amends

I'm out the door again;
But where am I going and where have I been?
I knew she would be there so why did I go?
I had to see her again that I do know.

It is all over and it is for the best.
There are so many words to get off of my chest.
I know that it was her smile that I craved.
But I must stay away I must be brave.

She has caused me nothing but pain.
I must move on; there's nothing to gain.
I must look and find another chance.
Find someone new to romance.

I'm desperate and powerless;
So I have to confess.
Track her down and ask her why.
Why not me? Why with that guy?

How do I go about making my amends?
I no longer want to be friends.
But I must act like the bigger person.
I need closure that is my reason.

Censor

All these people are going nuts trying to censor.
What I think we need more of is the parent factor.
Be there for your kids and teach them right from wrong.
Don't put all of your blame on TV or a song.

It's our responsibility to teach our kids right.
Teach them to have class and not to fight.
Teach them to read and teach them to do math.
Teach them to eat and to take a bath.

Have some guts and tell them what to do.
Don't be afraid if they get mad at you.
Our country is proud and our country is free.
This is the way it should always be.

If you are worried about what they see or hear,
Don't let your kids listen, don't let you kids near.
Teach your kids respect and not to cuss.
Put the responsibility back onto us.

Falling for You

You make me so happy; you make me smile.
Everything about you drives me wild.
Every day that I get to know you more,
I get excited and my feelings soar.

Sometimes I don't always know what to say.
You are touching my heart in every way.
I hope that I am doing the same thing, too.
Nothing I can do, I'm falling for you.

When I'm with you, I feel so complete.
I cannot believe it's only 4 weeks.
I love your friends and family, too.
Nothing I can do, I'm falling for you.

Child

Life can be cruel, and life can be tough.
It's never easy; it's always rough.
But that's what makes it worth its wild.
So get married and then have a child.

Once you have kids, I think you will see.
How lovely life can really be.
It will open your eyes and even change you.
Life will seem different, and life will seem new.

Now there's something more for you to think about.
All of your actions you'll now start to doubt.
Before you do anything, you'll think of them.
Making money will now be your biggest problem.

You'll want to give your kids the very best.
Your thoughts of life being cruel will be put to rest.
There's nothing more amazing that you will see.
With the birth of a child, you will be as happy as can be.

Together Forever

Every day that we are apart,
I feel a pain inside my heart.
I close my eyes and start to think.
I hope you appear but then I blink.

I feel that it was meant to be.
Together forever, just you and me.
I get a chill when I feel your touch.
I can't stand still I love you so much.

If only this wasn't a beautiful dream,
Together forever would be you and me.

Heart, Mind, and Soul

As I stand up and look in the mirror.
The picture now becomes much clearer.
But is it really me that I now see?
That's not how I look, can it be?

The way I look doesn't match the way I feel inside.
Which look is more important? I must decide.
I have a wonderful heart and a wonderful mind.
But my outside looks put me in a bind.

This world only cares about what they can see.
But it's what's on the inside that matters to me.
And I wonder if anyone thinks the same.
But who is it that deserves all of the blame.

I think at first glance it's the looks that we seek.
But try living with them for more then a week.
I think if you're looking for something long term.
It's the heart and mind and soul that must be firm.

Lucky for me I found all in one.
So the search for me is now done.
Inside and outside beauty I see.
But I wonder what she thinks about me.

Just Us Three

I wish that we were not apart.
Living without you scars my heart.
I know that soon we will be,
Together again, just us three.

Then all of our times will be wild,
For you, and me, and our child.
This is the thought that keeps me strong;
Every day and all week long.

All good things to those who wait,
It's more than love, this is fate.
So, my love, it won't be long,
Now we know our love is strong.

Love Conquers All

I look into your eyes, but you just stand still.
Your deep stare sends me an unbearable chill.
You do not listen to the words that I speak.
You just stand still holding tongue and cheek.

What is wrong? I cannot read your mind.
Happiness is the key, but love makes you blind.
Every time we speak, we just start to fight.
This just isn't healthy; this just isn't right.

We must do something we are starting to fall.
I thought that they say that love conquers all.
Do you still love me, and do you still care?
All of this pain, it just isn't fair.

Is it time to move on and find someone new?
I love you so much but there's nothing I can do.
I don't agree that love conquers all.
I think it's the pain that changes us all.

Love from Afar

I cannot explain the way that I feel.
My feelings for you I know are for real.
I know I should not be feeling this way.
You take my breath away day after day.

From the moment that our eyes first met,
I felt it then and I knew what it meant.
I have never felt it this strong before.
But it is from a far that I must adore.

Oh how I long for that special day,
To pick you up and sweep you away.
If only one dream of mine could come true.
I would spend the rest of my life in love with you.

Love of a Lifetime

Even when I was young, I knew what I wanted in life.
To have wonderful kids and a beautiful wife.
To always be there and help them in every way.
To tell them I love them every single day.

Just for the chance to watch the kids grow.
To be there for my wife in joy and in sorrow.
This is a dream that I prayed would come true.
I didn't think it could happen until I found you.

You make me so happy; you make me feel real.
I love you so much so here is the deal.
I will always be honest and always be true.
I promise to always be kind and considerate, too.

So let's look to our future and what it might be.
A big happy family is the picture that I see.
I love you so much so please take my hand.
We can make this all happen I know that we can.

Morning

Every morning when I arise,
I take a look into your eyes.
I want to tell you just how I feel,
To let you know my love is real.

I put my hand on to your thigh,
I hear you take a long deep sigh.
As I continue to move my hand,
You whisper to me, "That's all I can stand."

As my hand passes over your hips,
I move in for a romantic kiss.
But now instead I whisper to you,
"Good morning, honey, I love you."

My Favorite Season

Summer is the season I like the most.
So let's raise our glass and say a toast.
I love the sun shining down on my face.
When I feel the heat, my heart starts to race.

To spend all day sitting by the pool,
There with my friends staying cool.
Summer by far is the best time of the year.
I get in my car and hit that higher gear.

I go to the park and I play some ball,
A nice cold drink, refreshing and tall,
If I could choose one season to be,
I have to say it would be summer for me.

I Once Thought

I once thought that you were the one.
My love for you was all or none.
I remember the times we spent in the rain.
You made it hard for me to restrain.

I once thought that our love was so strong.
I can't believe that I was so wrong.
The feelings that still stir deep down inside,
Like the waves hitting the beach at high tide.

I now know what I needed to learn.
To give you my trust was my concern.
Looking at everything that I had to gain,
I don't think that you were worth all the pain.

Interview

What I hate the most is to have to wait.
Just sit here and wait to see my fate.
It's like time doesn't move it goes so slow.
I can't take this anymore I need to know.

I look at the phone and wait for it to ring.
I get so bored that I start to sing.
If this takes any longer, I'll lose my mind.
To do this to someone just isn't kind.

Now crazy thoughts race through my head,
Did I do everything right? What words were said?
I have a good feeling I did my best.
I wish they didn't interview the rest.

This is the job I need this one.
All of this waiting is not fun.
It's hard to think; it's hard to eat.
I think I wore out the bottom of this seat.

Should I stay here or should I go out?
I can't take this no more I need to shout.
What else can I do? I gave it my all.
Wait the phone's ringing it must be the call.

Never Again

I miss you so much and in so many ways.
When I get depressed, I think back to the old days.
I keep thinking that one of these days you will call.
Then I realize that will never happen; there's no chance at all.

Remember when we would sit by the pool and talk all day long.
I keep thinking about what happened and what went wrong.
I know that you really loved me underneath it all.
So what happened what caused the fall?

You would not budge you would not compromise.
Every word out of your mouth was nothing but lies.
It's too late now; you killed the trust.
In the world of romance, it's everything or bust.

I caught you and your hands were red.
How could you do that in our very own bed?
And you thought you could still be my friend.
How did you feel when I told you it was the end?

No more friends, no more lovers.
I hope that you regret it forever.
You blew out the flame that very day.
I'm so glad I sent you on your way.

One of a Kind

What would I do if you were not there?
I could not take it I would not dare.
Every day would just get worse.
A terrible nightmare, a terrible curse.

I start to think of your beautiful grin.
Your incredible eyes your silky soft skin.
Who would I talk to that would help me unwind?
There is no one like you—you're one of a kind.

So what would I do if you were not there?
No one to relax with, they could not compare.
I hope one day you will be there,
Not only at work, but everywhere.

Open Seat

Every single day I start to smile more.
My love is real and true down to the core.
I know now that my dream has come true.
I feel so lucky that I have found you.

But a beautiful woman is not all that I got.
I received a brand new family in the same shot.
A family that's open, a family that cares.
A family that can provide many different chairs.

By chairs I mean something that is very rare.
No matter your problem, they're always there.
To take time and listen and to help you out.
A family that laughs more than it shouts.

This is something that I have not seen before.
As soon as they met me, I was cared for.
I now feel that my life is complete.
The love of my life, a family, and an open seat.

Not What I Thought

When I was little, I thought I knew it all.
I thought I was in control and I could make the call.
I thought that I really understood life.
I knew that I wanted kids and a wife.

I felt I could do what I wanted; no one could stop me.
I could mold myself into who I want to be.
They say if I knew now what I knew then.
My life would be different. I know it would have been.

I say things happen for a reason.
Like life there's always a new season.
This one may be hot and the next may be cold.
My parents tried to build me like a mold.

Do what I say not what I do.
I'm sure your parents told you that crap, too.
The best way is to show by example.
In this world, if you don't move, you get trampled.

I got to where I am because of me.
But life is so different then I thought it would be.
I made so many bad choices. I was such a fool.
So if I could go back, I would stay in school.

Open Doors

What is it that I'm looking for?
All I see is door after door.
So which one is it that I should pick?
Should I take my time or should I do it quick?

A change of life is what I need to find.
So which door is it behind?
What went wrong how did I get here?
The path is foggy; I can't see clear.

I think I know what I want to do.
So which door should I go through?
This is my last chance. I must get it right.
I want to start my new life tonight.

When I close my eyes, I do see clear,
Where I want to be by next year.
I want a house and kids and a wife.
This is the door to a whole new life.

I believe I found it and picked the right one.
The life that I want has now begun.
To change your life and find what you're looking for.
Start over from scratch and pick a new door.

Regret

We dance all day and into the night.
Just to be happy and no longer fight.
We smile and we laugh and we think of the past.
I wish that time didn't go by so damn fast.

What happened to us, and what went wrong?
We were so young but our love was strong.
Do you ever think of how it might be,
If you had never bumped right into me?

Where would we be and who would we have met?
Did we fool ourselves and think that we were set?
I knew it for so long but I could not admit.
I missed my true love—she was the perfect fit.

Scream and Shout

Where is my mom; where's she now?
That day she left I knew that somehow.
My life would change but for the better.
But she left me nothing not even a letter.

How could someone do that to their son?
I remember early on we did all have fun.
So what went wrong and was it my fault?
These feelings I keep locked in my vault.

But now it's time to let them all out.
Sometimes I want to just scream and shout.
I don't even know if she's still alive.
But these are the things that give me my drive.

I will never act like that to my own.
That's not even in question it is well known.
I must admit I wonder if she still cares.
It's too late now though she wouldn't dare.

This is not something I normally talk about.
But there are million others like me that want to shout.
So parents make sure that you do what you can.
Don't be like my mother, she just ran.

Simply the Best

Tonight, my dear, it is my treat.
A drink, a movie, and something to eat.
Whatever it is that you want to go see.
With you by my side, I'm as happy as can be.

I lose track of time when I'm with you.
You're a special girl; I'm lucky to have you.
But don't forget that you are lucky, too.
There aren't too many men that do what I do.

I am always there to listen and care.
Everything I have I always share.
I'm pretty good looking, and I'm good in bed.
I'm sorry, my dear, but it had to be said.

It's always your needs I try to fill most.
That's why I feel the need to now boast.
Even if you know it, I'll tell you the rest.
I'm not just a good person I'm simply the best.

The One for Me

Every day that I look into your eyes,
I fall in love but then realize.
You do not feel the same as me.
I dream of our life and how it could be.

If only you would give me just one chance.
I'd pull you close to me and ask for a dance.
I'd show you just how nice it would be.
If you would only please pick me.

I know that I am not the best looking;
I have a big heart and you would love my cooking.
The feelings I have when I see you smile.
I lose my breath, and my heart beats wild.

My whole body shakes when I feel your touch.
You're always on my mind. I love you so much.
I know that you don't feel the same as me.
I can't help but think that you're the one for me.

Our Place

It's time to go so put on your blouse.
Let's go out to see our very first house.
I am so excited I just can't wait.
There is nothing more that I appreciate.

Baby, this really is a dream come true.
And it's your favorite color; it's baby blue.
I look in the fireplace and I see a log.
I picture the backyard and I see a dog.

It has a big garage for both of our cars.
It's only two blocks from our favorite bars.
Call all of your friends and get them here fast.
We'll throw a big party; it will be a blast.

I close my eyes because I'm still in shock.
Our house is the biggest one on the block.
I already said this but you feel it, too.
This truly is a dream come true.

These Three

You make a life from what you give.
That is the best way to live.
I have learned this from my wife's dad.
To always be there through good and bad.

To make others happy in sickness and health.
No matter their race no matter their wealth.
I have never met anyone like him.
He always seems happy; he never looks grim.

To never give up and always work hard.
To be a step ahead not caught off guard.
This I have learned from my very own dad,
As well as how to use a heating pad.

You only live once so enjoy your life.
I found happiness when I met my wife.
These three people have taught me so much.
I'm lucky to have the vision to see it as such.

Smell of Love

All of my dreams come true when I look at you.
I'm overjoyed, and I hope you feel it, too.
My family can tell by the way that I walk.
Everyone can tell by the way that I talk.

It is you, girl, and I'm in love.
Together just like a couple of doves.
And you just can't pull us apart.
Because it's too late once we start.

I love the way you smell. I love the way you feel.
My heart is bursting, baby, this is the real deal.
I feel like I am alive and kicking.
I think about you so much its sickening.

I think about my hand on your thigh.
Your love gives me a natural high.
When I tickle your body with a feather,
It's like springtime and dangerous weather.

The bed shaking and the blankets on the floor,
The neighbors are all knocking on the front door.
But they all know what it is that we're doing.
You can smell it in the air—it's love that's brewing.

Making love, baby, it's a beautiful thing.
It causes most men to go out and sing.
I want to lay you down and go places we've yet found.
Make incredible love with no worry about sound.

Under the Sun

I sit and I wonder how it would be,
To travel the world with so much to see.
But would I be able to take it all in?
What would I see first, where to begin?

Paris, France, or maybe England,
Germany, China, or even Finland
But would I understand truly how it must be?
What about their lifestyle could I really see?

I know that the world is a beautiful place.
But to understand their life you must not race.
To understand how they live I would need much more time.
Not to talk or interact just act like a mime.

Maybe then I will begin to see.
How different they are different from me.
And why it is that we can't act as one,
This wonderful planet under the sun.

Too Late

I look at the bottle and what do I think?
I want to throw it straight down the sink.
I can't do that now it's too hard to stop.
If only I was addicted to pop.

It takes such control to not take a sip.
It touches my tongue it touches my lip.
I feel it go down the back of my throat.
I lost all my cars, my house, and my boat.

I lost both my kids. I lost my whole life.
I lost my soul, my job, and my wife.
Looking at this, you would think I would see.
All of the damage it has done to me.

It's easy to say but so hard to do.
If you aren't careful, it can happen to you.
There's nothing left and it's too late now.
I look in the mirror and ask myself how.

To Be There

I finally feel, I finally see.
Happiness was always deep inside me.
Now I see it was always there,
For me to bring out and to share.
To do my best while I am here,
To show my loved ones that I care.
To start each day with a smile,
To find my love and drive her wild.

This is how I thought it could be.
I never thought it would happen to me.
Now I must do what I can.
Try to be that perfect man.

To always try to understand.
To always be there and take her hand.
To touch her heart and touch her soul,
To make her laugh and lose control.

To end every day and night with a kiss,
To spend our life in eternal bliss.
Then to grab her close and whisper in her ear,
"You mean the world to me. I love you, dear."

Together as One

The feel of your touch, the feel of your kiss,
The sound of your voice are all things I miss.
When you're not here, things just don't seem right.
It's just not the same when you're out of my sight.

When you come back, I want to hold you close.
Give you not just one kiss but a healthy dose.
Grab you tight and hold you all day.
You and me, baby, in the bed we will play.

All day and all night, just you and me,
Together as one we will now be.
We'll go for a walk and sit outside,
I said I don't care but I'm sorry I lied.

I need you so much when you're gone, I cry,
If I lost you forever, I know I would die.
I know how to keep you here but only one way.
Together as one we must stay.

What I See

I take a deep breath then I release.
I close my eyes and ask you please.
Please be kind and please be true.
Is this too much to ask of you?

Stop the games stop the lies.
No more yells and no more cries.
How can you make me feel like this?
I feel no love in your kiss.

Why would you just string me along?
One more chance then I am gone.
I must be crazy my friends say.
But they see her in a different way.

But I can see deep down inside.
That's what she will normally hide.
Hide from the rest but not from me.
But am I just seeing what I want to see?

True Love

I want to show you a side of me that you don't know.
I want us to take that step so we can grow.
If you never try, then there's nothing I can do.
But I hope you know that I do want you.

Just like you I am afraid to take that chance.
But I promise you a world full of romance.
Always there for you if ever you need me.
No matter the cost whatever it might be.

I'll be waiting for you always and I'll be here.
Every day and every night if you need me, I'm there.
But if for some reason my dream doesn't come true.
I respect your wish but I will always be in love with you.

Wish You the Best

Now that you are leaving I wish you the best.
You are one of the great ones better than the rest.
No matter what you do you will go far in life.
Any man would be lucky to have you as his wife.

You are so smart and thoughtful and oh so beautiful.
These are some of the things that make you so wonderful.
You have the most electric smile that I have ever seen.
You are such a nice person; you could never be mean.

If things don't work out and we don't stay in touch,
You will be in my thoughts; I will miss you so much.
I will remember your incredible eyes and your smile, too.
I have never met anyone as special as you.

Turn My Cheek

I grew up fast the choice was not mine.
It made me who I am so that is just fine.
I learned so much at such a young age.
My temper was bad I was full of rage.

I felt that life could be very cruel.
I learned that I was playing the fool.
Once I chose to turn my cheek,
My future no longer looked so bleak.

I took a step in the right direction.
Now I was looking for perfection.
It hit me and I knew that I could control.
If I worked hard, I would reach my goal.

No longer would I feel so depressed.
The feelings of rage I compressed.
Maybe my life really wasn't that crappie
Because I learned how to always stay happy.

Working as One

War after war, you would think that we learn.
But nothing changes the fire still burns.
All of the hurting and all of the pain,
The leaders of this world must be insane.

Why can't they sit down and make up a plan.
What's in the best interest of the common man?
Providing a future for all of our kids,
But the government sits back and continues to bid.

They all bid on something they all think they're right.
That's why it always ends up with a fight.
Instead they should shut up and start to listen.
And the world would be in a better position.

Will it ever change? This I don't know.
For our children's sake, I do hope so.
Could you image how the world might benefit?
All working as one; no longer separate.

Who I Am

Why is it so hard to make a big change?
Get my thoughts straight and then rearrange.
Make everything right that I think is wrong.
So I write my words down and create a new song.

Easy to write down but very hard to do.
To change my whole life into something brand new.
No matter how hard I try, it cannot be done.
So I guess I will always be the same one.

Perhaps that is just was meant to be.
The way we are comes very naturally.
So how do I change the person that I am?
Or do I just accept it and say god damn?

Will I Look Back 11

I close my eyes and I can see the past.
I didn't think so then but it really flew past.
But I never thought that I would look back.
It was common sense that I did lack.

Life was hard and I knew it all.
Hit after hit I stood tall.
But never did I think about what might be.
The future was one thing that I didn't see.

Here I am now 30 and married.
I thought by now I would be buried.
Things have turned out like they said it would.
I didn't believe them then; I didn't think it could.

Now that I'm older, I think about what they said.
I'm ready for the future the past is now dead.
I truly believe that I'm on the right track.
But 30 years from now, will I look back.